LOVE LETTERS FROM AN INSOMNIAC

evangeline

Lunar Ink Publishing

ISBN: 978-1-7328928-5-9

Love Letters from an Insomniac
Edition II

Copyright © Evangeline All Rights Reserved

No part of this publication may be reproduced, distributed, or transmitted in any form or by any means, including photocopying, recording, or other electronic or mechanical methods, without the prior written permission of the publisher, except in case of brief quotations embodied in critical reviews and certain other noncommercial uses permitted by copyright law. For permission requests, write to the publisher, addressed "Attention: Content Permissions," at the address below.

Lunar Ink Publishing

evangeline.author@gmail.com

Printed in the United States of America

Lunar Ink Publishing

Illustrated by Dandi Pratama

may these pages give you
strength, understanding, hope, release, and, of course,
butterflies
as you follow in the footsteps
of love and loss

ready

ready

When did I last feel alive?

I dream of days that will never come
& chase promises that were never spoken
I covet a life that won't make me feel any more whole
& wash my hands of the deliverance that has found
some kind of purchase within me
Incapable of noticing the difference between
salvation and sin
I denounce it all

Clumsily seeking something whose shape I do not recognize,
I've turned off the lights &
have become blind to a truth I perhaps wasn't ready to know
anyway

Lay me down to sleep already,
for my dreams are more comforting
than a future I'm not sure I deserve

one I'm not sure exists

ready

ready

How can you expect anyone to love you when you don't love yourself?

Easier said than done. I wish for it. I shut my eyes tight each night and beg for it to find me when I wake. I seek it when I'm on the street and in crowded coffee shops. I look for it in myself, too, but when I face the mirror, there's nothing looking back at me. No hoping, no lies, no prescription glasses can change the nothingness I see—and, yes, I have tried getting a new mirror . . . or two or three. I wish I could love myself as recommended. I want to feel it just as I see it in books because that exists. Right? It'd be hungry. Obsessive. Maddening with need and desire and burning from the torment of being apart for even a second—the *agony*! The desperation of it all. The bellyache. The loyalty. The knowing of my own worth and the burn-the-world-down belief in it.

I'd clothe myself in it day and night, I'd have it playing on repeat, and I'd memorize it so as to never lose it and to never, ever forget the sound of its call. I'd stop cursing myself for every misstep. I'd thank myself for my mistakes because I would finally be capable of loving myself and loving my destructive wishful thinking and my broken hopes and the crooked road I have walked chasing horizons I'd never find. And I bet I'd see something worthwhile in my reflection for once. I think I'd see something ready to be loved. God, I wish for it.

ready

what kind of secrets were told under this night sky?
how many stars listened
to the seductive whispers of lovers?
did the love they breathed somewhere between their lips and infinity
give birth to the heavens before me?

and you

I wonder if you're watching the same cosmos.
do you wander back to it each night, as I do,
longing and wondering and missing.
can you hear my voice?
it's soft, like the smallest wave kissing the shore,
for I told the stars of you
and asked them to send you; though,

I confess I do not know you

yet

I've dreamt of you and
on late nights when sleep evades me, I
have written you letters. So many that I've ran out of postage.
I told the stars of the shape of your eyes, the forgiveness
of your demeanor, the nurture of your voice, and the
sweetness of your kisses.

God, I hope they're sweet.

I told the stars of the way you'd come sweeping in,
unannounced and chasing away all doubt and emptiness.
I told the stars of you because I prayed they would form a constellation
just for us.

I wonder if you'll follow those stars
and find your way to the one
who has been waiting for you their whole life.

ready

Sad birds still have a song
They still take flight

> With wings wounded

> With winds wild

> With will withered

Sad birds still yearn for harmony
For a melody to ease
What little they have left
To find someone
Something

> Anything

With an ear trained enough to love
Even a sad song

Sad birds still have a song

So why is no one listening to mine?

ready

    Let's meet in a dream.
I'll be the one in the clouds, legs swinging into
pools of sunrise. Eyes kissed by the stars.

When you find me,
let's run away together.
We'll go wherever you take us;
somewhere far and unknown and perfect.

        You'll be loved there.

I'll make it so you don't remember a single moment when
you felt unwanted or unworthy.
I'll be your guiding light, your path home,
your safe haven,
for you are precisely as you should be
and I am enveloped in awe of you.

        Let's meet in a dream.
There in that place we will find endless days
of solace and you will be free.

          Promise to find me there
          and I will promise to gift you eternity.

ready

When you see me
See me

For I deeply wish to be seen.
Seen for the effort I put in each morning when, *God*, I wish I was in bed.
Seen for the tenderness I show to strangers.
Seen for confidence I struggle to carry.
Seen for the hopes I hold desperately.
Seen for the range of my joy and
Seen equally on days when laughter doesn't come easy.
I deeply wish to be seen

       In my nakedness

When all that I am is bare and raw and true and ugly;
When all that I am is something even *I* struggle to love.

I pray that the one who sees me

       And *really* sees me

Sees not ugly but
Someone trying.
Someone learning. Someone hurting. Someone growing. Someone
Beautiful.

When you see me

See me

And cherish the sight.

ready

Cup my face in your hands.
Capture my essence in your smile.
Fall deep into my eyes,
for, if you let them,
they will tell you everything.

As you fall,
as you see my past,
my fears,
my ugly 2 AM thoughts,
and my dark secrets,
you'll find a room deep in my chest.
It will be empty.
It always has been;
no one has bothered to open its door.
When you find the room I
built to house my loneliness,
don't ignore it like the others.

Take a torch,

a match, anything you can find

and burn it.

ready

Let me swim in your oceans,
Let me battle your demons and scale your mountains,
Let me see the parts of yourself that you hide
The parts of yourself you promise don't exist
Or that you claim died long ago
Let me pull down the moon and bend the earth to my will
Let me defy the gods and rewrite fate
Let me in
So I may bask in the glory of your skies
And be reborn.

leaping

leaping

my soul latched to yours

you held together parts of myself that
threatened to fade
the pieces of me that I knew became rearranged
and painted a picture so
hauntingly beautiful that I no longer
recognized what was before me
I was a stranger to myself
someone new and strange and wonderfully thrilling

I loved her
the me I saw through your eyes
it was like looking through stained glass
but I didn't know that I should not have fallen
in love with the broken shards that blocked my vision
and disrupted the scene

I only thought it was beautiful
I thought it was meant to be
I thought it was life itself

leaping

breathe my name within your curses and moans
  let me ride the waves of your sharp intakes and
  sink into the way you command the rhythm of
  my heartbeat, paralyzed by the ecstasy of it all as
  we lay bare and entangled in the night, this dark
  sky the only witness to the way we touch

        —*p e r f e c t i o n*—

let me feel your love in the tightness
of your grip and in the way you beckon shivers down
my spine in a seduction both forsaken and holy
breathe my name, demand my pleasure, and I am yours
in this moment / under this sky / under you

I   am   yours

leaping

I have never felt more vibrant
than in the cradle of your gaze

Nothing has ever held me so gently and yet
so fiercely that made me feel both like flying
and falling
all at once

There was a flame between us
ignited by youthful naivety or by the passion
only poets command—I did not know
I couldn't tell you if it was the warmth I sought
or the burn   —   the torment of it all
But the knowing didn't matter.
Why risk seeking deep enough to know
what lay beyond the sweet protection ignorant bliss provided?

For I have never felt more vibrant
than in the cradle of your gaze
And I'd follow you anywhere just so
I may feel the sensation
to both fly and fall
all
at
once

leaping

I was drunk
on the feeling of you,
but it felt less like drowning
and more like
I was finally able to breathe
more like you gave me one more thing
to make me stronger
one more thing
to make life so much more
intoxicating.
But if this truly is drowning disguised as fantasy—
if the waters sincerely are coming to drag me under—
I'd rather drown than continue breathing.
Given the choice, I'd always choose to
drown in your liquor and your toxins and your sweetness.
I would drown under the power of your kisses
and be reborn in the chaotic perfection
that is your love.

And that is what's the matter with me.

leaping

Lord, do I remember
The first time you made me cry

You did it without a shout,
Without a raised fist, without a bulging vein
Threatening to burst from fury
As if it took no energy at all
To pull me someplace so low.

I remember the shock
Was almost more powerful than my grief
But then grief swallowed that whole, too.
I played out scenes of our lives in that moment: past, present, and
Oh god, the future. I saw it all and
I wailed at it, screaming for the future I feared
To disappear
To not be real
To not be our fate
Why me?
Why us?

Lord, do I remember
The first time you consoled me.
You did it with more gentleness,
More kindness, more understanding than
I thought I deserved
So I believed it would be the last time.

Lord, do I remember
The first time I thought it was the last time.

leaping

                 Maybe one day all the stars will align.
                 On that day, perhaps you might just say

you love me.

                     For now,
       I'll settle for your smile and I'll find peace
           where I can because I believe
             happiness is meant for us.

      Maybe one day you'll feel this way for me, too.
              But today is not that day,
              for today feels exactly like

drowning.

          Drowning in a sea of our weaknesses
                  my regrets
          my love for you filling in my lungs.
     How could something so wonderful be so deadly?
           What I would give to see your hand
 push through the waters and save me from this death!

But instead,

                 I learn to swim.
               I'm not good at it;
          my head is barely above water
     but I'm swimming and I'll make it to your shores
               even if I drown.

                                                             But I won't

                                                                  right?

leaping

you were my poison
and my antidote
the raging river
and the bridge
the wind which guided my flight
and broke my wings in your tempest
I chased your path, my feet a slave to the trail
and yet I never found your footsteps
and I could never make it out of the labyrinth
my sanity now bound to my consequence
bound
to the rage and hopelessness and ugly and hurt and screaming into
nothingness just to be———*Ah,*

and then you kiss me
it's sweet as wild honey,
the gleam in your eye a beacon to a home long lost
my fears chased away
I've forgotten it all
I am whole

For now

withered

withered

                                          I have some regrets
I'll bury them under your bed
pretend that they're yours
so my room can stay clean
spotless
innocent
nothing like yours

I'll critique your space each time I visit
pointing out the dusty floorboards
the pillow that's out of place
the mess threatening to flood out from underneath your bedframe because

I know that mess
after all, it's mine

but I'll never admit that

not to you

I have no regrets
I've given them all to you
I feel free / weightless / spotless / innocent

are you really complaining about the weight?

You were never meant for love.
Your eyes were never shaped
to see the light within me.
Your hands weren't molded
to hold me as if losing me would kill you.
Your heart doesn't bleed
with passion over the thought of my presence.
You weren't meant for love;
it's what I've always believed.
But I was wrong.

You were.
You are.
Just not for me.

withered

you haven't known love
for quite some time.
for some time before I appeared:

Her.

this mysterious phantom made you feel love
& now she haunts me.
I am stalked by the knowing that there were once days
you gave her every piece of you &
consoled her with the same reassurances you gift me &
told her *she* was your one & only.

how did her smile make your heart race?
how did her touch make you feel safe?
how did the sound of her voice take you home?

how did her unruly nature push you
past the brink of sanity, and yet have you crawling back

for more.

were her colors more vibrant than mine?
was her madness more alluring than my peace?
& is she still there
in the back of your mind
gripping at your heart
tearing at your skin like an addiction?

do you still think of her

when the world is dark and I lay beside you?
is that when you think of the way

she used to kiss you?

withered

                              Lost.

                    Lost and crawling

         and struggling to make it out of the woods that are you.

Your branches snap in my face.

Your rocky paths trip my feet.

Your thorny bushes cut,

                                                                          leaving

                        me bloody.

           And yet each time I reach the brink of where you end,
              I smell the sweet scent of the flowers and berries
                     which hide within you.
                I recall the sunrise in your mountains
                that brought tears of joy to my eyes.
                I hear the gentle song of birds
                   that soar in your fields.

                    I'm sucked in again,
           cutting my own rope that was to save me
               from your beautiful ravines.

withered

I wonder why I never auditioned for the theatre
because the way I pretend you love me would
win a Tony. I write myself love letters read
aloud by your voice and signed with your name
at three AM when the knowing of your disinterest
in me grows too strong—and all too real—because
I refuse to accept it. I could rival Lea Solanga and
Ramin Karimloo with the performances I put on
when you tell me you still love me and I pretend to
believe it. Oh, how I play those moments over and
over again until I give the words the life you should
have delivered them with in the first place. *Cut!
One more time! From the top! But this time with more
feeling!* If I continue this dance, you'll eventually
cut in and the story can continue as if we never broke
pace to begin with. I'll keep painting pictures of your
smile that you once had in my presence. I'll keep
making excuses and hiding myself behind pleasantries.
I'll keep holding your body tight when you turn from
me in the night; when you move farther at each
instance of my touch. I'll just pretend you're asleep
and that you don't *know* you're moving away. I'll
keep apologizing and blaming myself because you
say I'm too defensive and maybe you're right; maybe
the real work starts with me. I'm sorry. *God! I'm so sorry*!
I'll keep telling myself to hold it together while gripping
tight to a bathroom counter and staring back at a face I
no longer remember while you sit playing nice with the
waitress—a wolf in sheep's clothing whom I hate and
am desperately in love with. I'll keep pretending it
doesn't hurt. I'll keep telling myself that love is hard,
but that it's worth it. I'll keep loving you and the love
story I cast myself in, even though I am no longer the
lead. I'll keep pretending even if

it's the end of me.

withered

I'm trying.
What that means is
I'll rip my heart out. Here it is.
I'll give it to you.
Please don't mind the holes and the dents and the scars.
They come from caring too much
for those who would rather live without me.
They come from the countless times I've cried *I'm sorry*
& Oh, God, please forgive me. I didn't mean to.
That wasn't my intention. I only want to love you. Please,
love me back.

They come from the hurtful words you said
and me trying to sew the wounds by saying
it was all my fault.
I'm trying.
What that means is
I'll cry myself to sleep for days.
I'll hide myself in the darkness
under my covers
under the weight of what haunts me
under the weight of the words that won't stop ringing.
I'm a mistake.
Am I sick?

God, but I'm trying!
I desperately pull but you push
opposite directions—a friction that rends which means
I'm tearing myself to shreds just for the chance to hear you say
you don't hate me
Because I no longer feel desired by you.
What about that is too much to ask? What about me is not enough?
Am I losing my sanity?
Have I have been stripped of all that I am
to shape myself into the woman you'd want?
I am a shell of whom I once was, but even that
I'll give to you.

withered

Dear friend/my younger self/to whom it may concern,

Oh dear, sweet thing, I wish my words meant something to you, but I know you do not hear me, too consumed by the all-encompassing sound of your own heart breaking and the violent echoes of the last words which fell from their lips. I wish I could console you. I would tell you that you can take that pain, hold it in your hand, and crumple it like paper, like it was weightless, nothingness, insignificant. That the heat from the rage you hide could ignite that paper, and that you could be rid of it with something as simple as your own will.
Oh dear, sweet thing. I wish I could stop your heart from breaking. I wish I could give you my strength.
I'd wither so that you may breathe.

-a powerless observer

withered

      I held close to you
        for your smile,
     your calming touch,
       the stability,
          for you.
       I clung to you
   because for some reason
every inch of me screamed
    that I loved you and
     you loved me, too.

                        Yet you broke me.

You held me as I crumbled,
pretending nothing was wrong,
       kissed my neck
      and, all the while,
drove a knife into my back.

withered

You're eight thousand miles away
You'd think that would wrap you around the earth and
bring you right back

                    close   to   me

but I cannot seem to find you
Even when I touch you I question
if   you're   even   really   there?

Eight thousand miles and yet
I still chase the distance,
each step trying to re-lay our foundation,
planting, like seeds, those early mornings of
being wrapped in each other's arms,
legs tangled,
every inch of each other pressed
as tight as we could manage
and lips tracing every inch of our skin
But the soil is not fertile and our love
does not grow here
Not when you're eight thousand miles away

Not when my legs aren't meant to tread that distance

Not when you'll be eight thousand and one miles away by the end of the day

withered

Your hand was a promise
A promise that we
Didn't have to face our demons alone
A promise that the same fingers
Which entwined with mine
Would also raise me up
And believe in me
They would love me
But you didn't want to take my hand

You didn't like the touch

Please see through this smile;
it has become so heavy
and exhausting to carry.
Please see the pain in my eyes.
I am screaming for you,
I'm just too afraid to speak.

Take me in

chase away the darkness
that has made a home in my heart
light a candle
and love me in the shadows of my melancholy

withered

> When he left,
> the door swung wide open.
> I was too weak
> or too broken to close it.
> Winds whipped and howled
> and the warmth of my dying fire
> attracted what he promised I would never find:

Loneliness.

> When The Lonely crept in,
> it made itself at home.
> It propped its feet on the couch as the last
> ember of my fire burned out.
> And when I went to bed,
> The Lonely followed.
> It curled in beside me,
> but I only felt shivering cold.
> As the clock ticks,
> I feel we are not so different,
> The Lonely and I.
> In fact, we are the same.

> And The Lonely keeps me warmer
> than you last did.

withered

                       the cycle doesn't end with my name

and that's what hurts me the most
there will be another
& there will be more after that
a candy trail of broken hearts / broken bodies / broken will
you will find another to believe in you
someone else who will be too entranced
by your admittedly spectacular view to see the impending doom
lurking behind the sweet nothings you expertly deliver

                  trapped in a glass cage

I'm banging against a wall no one can see
screaming warnings no one will hear
warnings that will be written off as hysteria
                poor thing

you'll advert your gaze
my throat will bleed
                raw from the ruin of my experience

another already following in my footsteps

what a pity
       what a shame
              what a waste

that is what I hate you for the most

let me fall to my knees / so that I may
beg properly   release me
your talons are sharp as ever as you
impale into my consciousness / even
after all these years it is my dreams you
terrorize / even after all these years there
is still a part of me which clings to you—
out of hatred and disgust and regret, yet
still attached to you—an ever-present
awareness of your evil / yet you are
alluring in my dreams / a tide which
raptures me deeper though I cannot hold
my breath for long / even if I wrench
myself from you —from this all-too-real
hellscape   and   dreamland   you've
forsaken me to / *pinch me! wake me!* /
a power pulls me nearer / I am too weak
to fight it / I always have been / some
things never change / like getting closer
to   holy   flames   or   being   drug
underground / you usher me to death
               release me
I do not want this / I wake with blood
pooling in my mouth / despair staining
my cheeks / wretched chills devouring
whatever part of me remains from your
wreckage / a vile burn from where you
dared reclaim my body
leave me
I beg of you spare me from the sight of
your face and from the remembrance of
your touch / let me fall to my knees / I'll
gift you with your favorite view as a
parting gift, let you see me a final time
weak   and   begging
please accept this olive   branch
so that my mind may finally know peace
/ from you

withered

worthy

worthy

           Why does my body not decompose?
              Why am I not hidden
             under the impossible weight
                of wet tissues

hours of crying
hours of wishing
hours of missing

        and crumbling under the knowing
      that I will never feel your arms around me again?
    I felt my foundation tremble in anticipation of catastrophe.
     The very essence of who I am teased disaster and yet . . .

        why have I shed no tears for you?
        I shed so many while we were in love.
          Perhaps it is because

the rage

          you painted me with

gave birth

         to the realization that

I   don't   need   you.

worthy

I used to want to be delicate
because that's what you liked.
delicate was soft / cute / welcoming.
it wasn't a threat.

> I used to want to be pretty.
> pretty because people like pretty.
> pretty doesn't yell / doesn't cry / doesn't complain.

I used to want to be nice and calm and quiet and whatever version of what good
looked like for you that day because that meant I was good, too.

> now

> I want to be unburdened.
> unburdened because maybe it wouldn't hurt so much.
> because then maybe I wouldn't remember.
> because then maybe I wouldn't care.

I want to be strong
because of you
because of you and people like you
who haunt people like me

> I want to be free.
> I want to be free of the feeling of your hands
> on my waist / my arms / my throat
> free of remembering how it felt
> the fear   the weakness   the blistering of my tears

I want to be courageous
courageous because you don't deserve the power you have
how dare you train good people to cower?
how dare you extinguish someone's will?

> I want to be uninhabited of the memory of you
> and emerge knowing that I am no lesser
> for the nightmare you put me through.

today I'm ditching the pretty, trampling the delicate, and foregoing all niceties.
today I'll be Strong / Courageous / Unburdened / Uninhabited / Free.

You are not broken
beyond repair.
You are not someone
who needs to be fixed.
You are someone who needs
to be believed in;
if not by another person,
then by you.

worthy

I could easily live in a room
built of my past.
I would swim in my memories,
drink my regrets,
and then surely collapse
under the pressure of the fears I fabricated.
But I much prefer the sunlight
where self-loathing doesn't eat me alive,
for instead
I can live unshackled.
Unbound by lies and traps and disgust.
I much prefer to burn that room

And dance in its ashes.

worthy

I may not be the liquor you crave
But I am the nourishment souls thirst for

I may not be sticky sweet or
Go down like a fire that keeps you warm and burns just enough
To make you feel alive

But you won't taste regret in your mouth
The next morning—sour and pitiful and brimming with
Good intentions gone rotten and loud sirens ringing in

Emptiness

—When it's my presence you seek

Though, this knowledge is not a weight on
My shoulders. I'll still sleep soundly tonight.

I don't need to be the liquor you crave

For I am already the nourishment that quenches my soul

worthy

When I returned to myself
I stood at the door with the porch light on.
I had hot food on the table, wine poured, and a fresh set of clothes

                 Clean from the ruin of my heartache.

When I returned to myself
Soul music filled the space where pain once resided.
Logs were burning in the fireplace, a bath was drawn, and I gave myself a hug

                 Warmer than anything I've ever known.

When I returned to myself
I left the door unlocked and windows open because in this freedom I was *safe*.
Sticky notes littered the walls, telling me all the parts of myself that deserved to be

                 Free and adored and healed.

When I returned to myself
I fluffed the pillows and laid myself on Egyptian Cotton.
I no longer felt too small and diminished by someone else's shadow. I no longer
Felt shame for the loud space I took in rooms to make up for the feebleness which
Weakened me. I shed myself like a snake of guilt and loathing and the ever-
Pestering question of if I'd ever be enough because Lord knows

                 I was always worthy of the love that had been denied me.

When I returned to myself

worthy

Sometimes
I forget that I am loved

So that I may count the reasons I deserve to be

And fall in love with myself
Over again

Vanity is a slur I'm proud to wear
A slur I fought to feel worthy of
And it has no true name but

Realization

Its surname

Worthiness

I fled once.
Afraid to give in,

To let myself know love for oneself
To know comfort

In my skin
Within my body
Within my mind
With fear and fearlessness alike

To know my truth
My path
My face and heart

Sometimes
I forget that I am loved
So that I may swim in the gospel which sings

Love is what I am

worthy

I am an ocean.
Beautiful or treacherous,
no one can decide.
My waves are massive.
Even in clear waters, hurricanes linger.
But, please,
do not fear me.

Brave my depths!

Navigate my blue waters
and pass all my demons.
In that journey

you'll find that my heart
is Atlantis.

And, if you want,
you can make a home there.

beloved

beloved

I met you on a night so dark it made you believe you'd be swallowed
whole. A blackness so monstrous yet fateful it'd steal away every trace of you—no
clues, no evidence
your head was cast down, eyes scanning the cobbles at your feet
breath tight, holding in the heart you thought would surely crumble to pieces
if you lost concentration for even a moment

you weren't looking, so it was only I who noticed the constellation above
and how the glow cast lovely, deep rays of light on your face and
dark shadows just as perfect, for when you glanced up, those dark shadows
bore way for the most breath-taking contrast, laying itself a canvas for the spectacle
that are your eyes
and when your eyes met mine . . . I stumbled. My feet locked, lungs paused, heart
fluttered. The night which surrounded us in that second exploded into light and
I felt something holy

knowing you now, I know that you were stalked by darkness and an anguish
so deep I would have been foolish to try and remedy
and yet
I did not see scars nor weakness nor despair

I saw you

I saw you and felt blessed to behold such radiance, holding my breath until dawn
when you would surely rapture me once more in the beauty that has always
worshipped you
even on nights so dark you believe they could swallow you whole

heartbreak had found you, and yet

so had I

beloved

I felt you in a way that was
Shocking and delightful and blissfully unsettling
Just like the first chord of music in a silent room
I was not looking for you
I did not need you
Though I'd be damned if I said
I did not want you
All the same, there you were
Here you are
That first chord of yours
Disrupted my symphony of disbelief
And orchestrated something lovely and altogether unfamiliar
Your sound made me stop
Made me think
Made me feel hope
And—though I did not know it—would
Alter the course of my life

I was stunned
If this was the melody that would accompany my path
I was willing to listen
I wanted to discover our harmony

beloved

She had never been loved / deeply, immensely loved.
Not the way she deserved. Not the way I longed to.
Not the way I would tear down monuments to ensure it.
When I was with her, I breathed for the first time.
I saw her trembling waves and longed to be rocked by the
rhythm of her ocean. I witnessed the storms she hid beneath
her surface and they empowered me to be someone more than
I was yesterday. In the sadness she swore she did not feel—
my brave soldier—I only saw her great capacity for love.
The way she took all that she was, wrapped it with a bow, and
gifted it to everyone she met, sacrificing a piece of herself each
time and never asking for anything in return, she may have been
too terrified of casting herself a burden or beggar. She may
not have believed it was possible for her to receive it at all.
I watched those pieces leave her one by one, each claiming her
until she felt withered, and then she gave some more. God,
did she have love to give and it was a gift the world
did not appreciate nearly enough.

She had never been loved, tenderly / unconditionally loved.
Perhaps that is what I was born to do.

beloved

if I could build a garden
out of the life that waits within you,
I would never run out of flowers.
I'd keep your soil rich, mastering the science
of the exact sunlight you need, and
I'd nourish you with the purest of water.
your herbs would make remedies to heal the most fatal of diseases,
and the sight of you would make hardened souls turn to devotion.
I'd line every path, every sidewalk, each highway
with the flowers that bloom within your soul.
and then, perhaps, the world could finally love you
as I do.

beloved

    She was shelter from the storm
                  and yet
            the hand which brought you
                  to dance in the rain.

        Life poured from her fingertips
          and beauty was born
              from the grace of her smile.

    When one falls in love with the world
            as she had,
one becomes the sun, the moon, and the stars above.

        Oh, celestial wonder,
        you showed me how marvelous it is
              to fall in love
                  with yourself.

beloved

She is the kind of art
one studies in awe.
I wish I could take all her broken parts
and piece her back together like a mosaic.
I would show her the complexity of her yellows,
the life in her greens,
the depth in her purples,
the passion in her reds,
and the harmonies within her blues,
so exquisite
they bring tears to my eyes.
I would show her that the jagged edges
are nothing but the road which
led me to her
and her to me.
I would make her step back and
fall in love with how her colors dance
just as I have.
I wish she could feel
the life she has breathed into me
and experience all the colors
that live through her.

beloved

Your fingers trace prophecies on my skin
I hold my breath as the stories take form
Promises of your love
Promises of the road ahead
Promises that your fingers will keep roaming until they explore
Every part of me
And then go again

I never believed in fortunes and fates
But now my world spins on the axis of this prophecy
I'd sacrifice myself for this belief
My sun rises for it and my tides are pulled by its power
My very existence hangs on your every word
And, God, do I trust it
For you make my world feel like a better place
And you don't make me question if I deserve it

beloved

You dipped a brush in blackness
    And covered the plain, lonely white that was my existence
You called the dark strokes on the canvas my misery
        But said I needn't fear it
        That I needn't feel shame
        You said it allowed the other colors to breathe
    You made me believe misery was necessary and lovely and important, too

You whispered my name
    And the stars ignited
Love fell from your lips as you spoke
        Of my laughter and the sanctuary of my touch
        And I bathed in it until your declarations felt real and within reach
        Then I asked to hear the words once more

You painted the infinite I knew
        With the vibrancy you said you saw in my eyes
And then you sealed it within a kiss
    And gifted it to me

                A revival / A promise / A sweet awakening

beloved

I look at love differently because of you.
I once used it lightly, handing it to random people who I thought wanted to hear it. To people who may give me something in return if they liked the flow of the words enough. Love was meaningless, a tool, and, though, I was slow to admit it, I was sickened by myself and by the way the words I believed in so much could feel so empty. But when you burst through the door, it was like an eclipse. My world was normal, and then dark and terrifying and a spectacle that made me question all I had written myself to believe. And when I felt the world slipping away beneath my feet into darkness, you ushered in the day. You flooded everything I knew with light and shone on love in a way I had forgotten it could be illuminated. It was like I was a child once more—free and unknowing of the harm that would undoubtedly befall me, or perhaps I was not unknowing of it but for the first time in so long, I was no longer afraid. I began seeing love in the way the smell of coffee fills a home. Love greeted me in the street, waving hello, and for the first time, I waved back. I recognized love during a daytime rain and how the sunlight seeped through the clouds afterwards, casting diamonds on the dew it left behind—dew I once hated to get on my shoes. I felt love during morning commutes, in waking and feeling well-rested before my alarm went off, and in things so simple as perfectly buttered toast. I was awakened to the possibility of it, and I began to pursue it. Love was a frequent visitor—no longer a stranger whose name I pretended to know. And yet, all those moments pale in comparison to the kind of love I seek most.
And that is within every moment I am with you. When I look back on my life, I will recall every good memory as a memory where you are at the forefront. And when people think of me when I am gone, they will also think of you and the love you delivered to not only me but to the way I saw the world and the world was able to see me.
I look differently at love because of you and now it finally wants to look back at me.

beloved

beloved

I felt you so powerfully
my whole body shook.
You were all my lips
could pronounce;
all my mind and heart knew.
You were a divinity that graced my mortality
with a life too spectacular to comprehend
and yet too precious to abandon.
If I could take you
and lift you into the heavens
to show you the wonders that live there,
I would scream,

"This is the love you have given to me!"

I would make your very existence tremble
as you have made mine.

beloved

I knew you were meant for me
        because I have known you before.
When we met
                our souls were no strangers to each other
                and each conversation, each kiss, was like a greeting from
a memory of lives we already lived, promises made by old lovers who vowed that
                      they'd find each other again.

I have seen you before
        in the rays of sunlight illuminating a church's stained glass

I have felt you before
                in a dream painted in the colors of my loneliest desires
              and yet drenched in my lust
                            longing finally answered.

I've been surrounded by you before
        in a garden you must have unknowingly planted for me,
     thinking that someone, somewhere would appreciate your labors.
            Well, here I am
            in awe.

I have heard you before in laughter
        and felt you in the desperate anticipation
            of a lover's kiss.

I have loved you before
        and I knew that the moment our eyes met.

        I have loved you before,

            I will love you again,

And I will love you a thousand times more.

beloved

You were my apothecary.
Each time the bell dinged as I walked through your doors
Was a reminder that I would be okay
Your embrace was medicine to my broken soul
Your words like prescriptions for a better tomorrow
Who knew that your kiss could heal a hope
I had abandoned long ago.

But I am no greedy patron.
I yearn for your remedies—needy and insatiable, yes—and yet there I am
Clearing your bottles of cobwebs,
Washing your windows. Cleaning up the messes
Others left behind.
For every breath of life you feed me,
I stretch myself to repay you tenfold,
Careful not to overdo my doses . . . though, I'd happily take you all
Just for the chance to be brought back to life
By you.

I'll always return here
To my apothecary
When the doors have weakened on their hinges, when the register is more dust
Than cash, when the owner has lost hope and paint begins to fade

There I will be,
Smiling on the sidewalk, waiting for the open sign to light
Hopeful and patient and grateful for
My sweet apothecary.

beloved

                      spiders   /   snakes   /   heights
                      burning   /   suffocating   /   falling

My greatest fear   is living in a world without you in it

Setting the table with only one plate
Movies in isolation
Sunsets in solitude
Only making one side of the bed

            But that's not true because I'm a messy sleeper
            I could never keep both sides tidy &
            You always loved that about me

I have a fear of one day learning how to make a home that's much less a home
                                                                  because you're not there

So, tell me—*please, if anyone is listening!*—how do I make this last?
How do I make a mortal enemy of time

                          & win.

How do I ensure this era has no end? That each night is greeted by morning?

I'll throw sheets over clocks & destroy my watches if that'll make time stop
I'll always keep two plates on the table
I'll build things that last & become a master carpenter to repair what tries to break
I'll climb great heights, wade through seas of spiders & snakes, I'll be not afraid
Of fire nor deep waters
I'll fall fatal distances
I'll breathe fire / flood deserts / topple mountains / perform impossible miracles
I swear
        I'll try

Because if I believe hard enough & fight & love & stay strong for you
For us
For me
I'll never have to worry about living in a world without you in it.

                                                                  Promise?

beloved

        Whisper while I dream
so that your soft words may craft
worlds only our hearts know.
May the gentle touch of you pulling me close,

careful not to wake me,

paint a sunrise.
May the even rise and fall of your chest
give chase to the breeze
which carries the smoky scent of your skin.
May I always wake beside you
in the dead of night
when the moon caresses your face
or in the early break of day
when the sun greets us with her warmth.
May it always be you.

gone

gone

You existed in spring
when life not only
blossomed throughout the earth,
but within me.
You wrenched away sorrows that plagued me
as if they were weeds
and watered hope that had long since withered.
When summer came,
and I stretched toward the sun,
your eyes never left me.
You said you had never seen
anything more splendid,
and in that truth
I bloomed.

gone

I reach for you
in the spaces far and in between.
The light your soul brings
is the homing signal
that leads me back into your arms.
And though there are times
that we are so far
and I feel hopelessly lost,
I always find my way
back to you.

vapor hangs on the glass
letters etched in the fog   your name
the sound of my finger running along the window—
a pathetic moan, a sad friction—
until my sorrow warps the piercing noise into
something sweeter
until my delusion disguises the noise
into the sound of your heart beating, the

thump-thump, thump-thump

I can still hear it if I close my eyes tight enough and
trick myself into believing that
my head still rests on your chest
fabricated sincerity deceivingly perfect

thump-thump, thump-thump

as the fog clears
my written note fades, my letter on glass
forgotten, unheard. No!
frantically I rewrite it
a g a i n and a g a i n

thump-thump, thump-thump

for on rainy days
it is the only way my body knows

thump-thump, thump-thump

that your heart will come back
to mine

thump-thump, thump-thump

gone

> My body burns a little more
> each day that you are gone.
> I fear that when you return,
> if you ever do,
> there will be nothing left of me
> except for ashes so inconsequential
> that even the weakest breeze
> could blow me away.

gone

If I could fill the holes in my heart
that you made when you left,
maybe the sun wouldn't be so cold.
Maybe this bed wouldn't feel so empty.
But, for now, I shall fill those holes
with thoughts of you.
They bring me comfort at night
when the darkness reminds me

you   are   not   here.

gone

        I remember you
                with a song and how you moved
                ever so clumsy when it played.
Sometimes I see your face
                in a stranger's
                and it steals my breath.
                My mind,
            whether it be a blessing or a curse,
              constructs you in a dream;
            that's when I know you clearest,
                but it's too much to bear.

                I can still recall
            how your lips upturned in a smile,
                but, at times,
          I forget the sound of your laughter.

Please forgive me.
I never meant for this.

                If this was the divine plan,
                    then God is cruel.

                The earth has you now.

                I only have the memory.

I know you in times gone by

gone

In nights wrapped in deep oranges and reds and
Browns and 70s film granularity
Warmed by a fire
And the sound of your voice, seeping
Through the house, hanging on every door and picture frame,
Lingering in the walls,
Making home in the very essence of who I am

When I close my eyes
I'm there
I can feel it.
The colors become so real
Until they are breathing and I am—

                              Not

I smell the cologne
The food left on the counter
The old, wooden frames
I'm there

And yet

No matter how fast
Nor how desperately
I chase it
I can never get close enough to capture what once was ours
I'm always just a   b r e a t h   too far away

So I know you in those times too distant
For me to hold
I know you there for but a moment until it

v a   n   i   s   h   e   s

gone

I woke one night,
desperately grasping at the sheets, soaked in sweat
and tears, uncomfortably heavy from the
relentless ache in my chest. The moon illuminated
the bed; its rays silhouetting the lovely shape you
once took beside me. If I stared long enough, I
would fall into a trance.

The moon was once witness to our ecstasy
but now is a witness to nothing but a
despairing widow. I look to her still, the
moon. Her lights dance and play tricks and
I could almost see your smile.
I could almost remember how it felt to roll
over and fall perfectly into your embrace as
if you had been waiting for me all along. At
night, the moon and I would tell each other
of the love we knew. And then, as we spoke
like old friends, the moon and I, when my
lips only knew the sound of your name and
when my body only recognized the warmth it
once felt, I could almost pretend my heart
hadn't died.

gone

my memories of you
are the stone steps
that lead to the home
you built for me in your heart.
and there I will wait for you
always

tomorrow

tomorrow

My consciousness fills spaces that are not one nor the other
Here nor there
Known nor cryptic
I've drawn maps that lead to what awaits me
But in this place I've found no atlas with an exact end
& I must admit
I find freedom in that perplexity
Thus I have committed myself to days that are not known & time
That is not numbered, for hasn't time not already been enough of a thief
Of years that feel barely lived?

So when you look for me
Find me where today seeps into tomorrow
Where lightning strikes ground
Where the sea meets the stars
Where music fades to wind
I am the atmosphere that surrounds you &
The Earth which steadies you
I am spaces both distant & near
Dreaming & awake
Tranquil & soaring
In this nowhere & everywhere
Floating in an expanse that is not quite real, yet close enough to feel you
I am with you

I have always been with you

tomorrow

I see you—stranger—and think of the life you lived
the people you loved, the days you desperately hold to when all else seems to
slip away
I think of a loneliness and bitterness that I pray does not attach itself to you
I wonder if you're happy

I wonder if someone loves you and when the last time was that someone called
you beautiful / handsome / special
I wonder if you still feel vigor
if you feel that there's still plenty of life left to live
and if you then seek it / live it / never let it go
I hope people are kind to you
I hope they hold open doors and show patience when the world seems to be
spinning faster than you last remembered it
I hope the world is good to you

because you were young once
and we'll catch up to you
and we also will sit in the days where all we can think about is
when we were young once, too

tomorrow

mourn for who you used to be.
build a memorial for days long past,
for love once known,
a body once treasured.
build it a space where it can live
and visit it.
bring it flowers,
tell it stories, and
pour it whiskey.

mourn for what you once had
but never forget that who you are in this moment
deserves more love than the past.

ABOUT THE AUTHOR

Well-traveled and with an adventurous soul, Evangeline loves how romantic it is to dive into a story and discover a new world. She hopes that not only will her writing transport readers to somewhere terrific, but it will also help others gather strength, courage, confidence, and a love for themselves and the world.

tomorrow

there is something so lovely
about yearning for your own existence

there is something so healing about
waking up with a belly full of rage
a mouth full of regret
legs limp with distress
hands full, holding agony like water

        endlessly overflowing

how does one endure?

and yet

still yearning for that first breath when you wake
knowing that you made it through the night
seeking the sunlight peeking through your blinds,
unparalyzed by the memories which afflict you;
venturing out and trying again
with a reckless abandon
loving the life that was given to you time and time again
despite . . .

   . . . despite knowing you may lack the fortitude

I will dare myself to be so brave
I will dare myself to love what once scared me

tomorrow

An Open Letter to Hope

Hello, stranger,
Where have you been? Foregoing directions and
Forging your own path?
Taking twisting routes along treacherous mountain paths?
Stopping at each outlook to soak in the view?
Strolling down dreamy, small town main streets as you
Continue your odyssey?
It's not about the destination, after all, but the journey—however;

                                  I was your destination
And you took your sweet time finding me

So   finally   hello, stranger

I've heard of you; crafted my own idea of your company and
Kept a key under my door mat so you'd always have a way home
Loyal to your inevitable return, I always kept the guest bed tidy
With a candle lit to welcome you when you arrived,
Likely weary and needing of rest
I've been waiting for you
                        Here you are at last

                But I have grown old   in both body and spirit

Will you help me, new friend, as I attempt to brave tomorrow?
My legs have grown weary and my heart too heavy
I feel as though I am but a b r e a t h away from turning to dust
But I am not ready yet
So, stranger, new friend, Hope
If I believe in you,

Will I make it to sunrise?

www.ingramcontent.com/pod-product-compliance
Lightning Source LLC
Chambersburg PA
CBHW021627080526
44585CB00013BA/906